Growing
Annuals

Growing Annuals

WRITER
ANNE M. ZEMAN

PHOTOGRAPHERS
ALAN COPELAND
AND BARRY SHAPIRO

ILLUSTRATOR
JAMES BALKOVEK

AVON BOOKS  NEW YORK

Product Manager: CYNTHIA FOLLAND, NK LAWN & GARDEN CO.

Acquisition, Development and Production Services: BMR, Corte Madera, CA

Acquisition: JACK JENNINGS, BOB DOLEZAL

Series Concept: BOB DOLEZAL

Project Director: JANE RYAN

Developmental Editor: KATE KELLY

Horticulturist: BARBARA STREMPLE

Landscape Design and Horticultural Consultant:
   RG TURNER JR

Photographic Director: ALAN COPELAND

Art Director (cover): KARRYLL NASON

Art Director (interior): BRAD GREENE

Cover Design: KAREN EMERSON

Cover Stylist: JOANN MASAOKA VAN ATTA

Cover Photo: BARRY SHAPIRO

Interior Art: JAMES BALKOVEK

North American Map: RON HILDEBRAND

Site Scout: PEGGY HENRY, RG TURNER JR

Photo Assistant: LISA PISCHEL

Copy Editor: JANET VOLKMAN

Proofreader: LYNN FERAR

Typography and Page Layout: BARBARA GELFAND

Index: SYLVIA COATES

Color Separations: PREPRESS ASSEMBLY INCORPORATED

Printing and Binding: PENDELL PRINTING INC.

Production Management: THOMAS E. DORSANEO, JANE RYAN

First Avon Books Trade Printing: February 1993

Library of Congress Cataloging-in-Publication Data:
Zeman, Anne M.
   Growing annuals / writer, Anne Zeman;
   photographers, Alan Copeland and Barry Shapiro,
   illustrator, James Balkovek.
      p. cm. – (NK Lawn & Garden step-by-step visual guide)
   Includes index.
      ISBN: 0-380-76800-3
      1. Annuals (Plants) I. Copeland, Alan. II. Shapiro,
Barry. III. Balkovek, James. IV. Title. V. Series.
SB422.Z46 1993
635.9'312--dc20   92-20458
                                                        CIP

Special thanks to: Katherine Kirk; Janet Pischel; the Henry Family; Roger Raiche; UC Berkeley Botanical Garden; Golden Gate Park, and Strybing Arboretum & Botanical Garden; Berkeley Horticultural Nursery; Blake Estate, UC Berkeley; Cynthia Egger; Galen Fultz; Patricia Posner; Mill Rose Inn, Half Moon Bay, CA; San Benito House, Half Moon Bay, CA; Sonoma Mission Gardens, Sonoma, CA; Blooms Nursery, Glen Ellen, CA.

Additional photo credits: Saxon Holt, pgs. 20–21, 25 (Next), 42–43; Jane Grushow/Grant Heilman, pg. 68, hyacinth bean; Derek Fell, pg. 69, moonflower.

Notice: The information contained in this book is true and complete to the best of our knowledge. All recommendations are made without any guarantees on the part of the authors, NK Lawn & Garden Co., or BMR. Because the means, materials and procedures followed by homeowners are beyond our control, the author and publisher disclaim all liability in connection with the use of this information.

AVON BOOKS
A division of
The Hearst Corporation
1350 Avenue of the Americas
New York, New York 10019

AVON TRADEMARK REG. U.S. PAT. OFF.
AND IN OTHER COUNTRIES, MARCA
REGISTRADA, HECHO EN U.S.A.

92   93   94   95   96   10   9   8   7   6   5   4   3   2   1

TABLE OF CONTENTS

THE PLEASURES OF ANNUALS

ALL-SEASON COLOR

Quick and easy to grow, available in a multitude of colors and sizes and tolerant of a wide range of soils, annuals are favorites of beginning and experienced gardeners alike.

Often blooming continuously for months, annuals provide an entire season of color. They come in every shade known to the flower world. Annuals bloom for only one season, allowing you to change the color and design of your garden each year.

Annuals are exceptionally versatile. They are excellent for massed plantings in formal beds or as edgings in sweeping curves along walks or driveways. Set them in a perennial border for all-season color or against shrubs and evergreens to add a dazzling accent.

Annuals are ideal in containers on a patio, terrace or poolside. Some trail, making them perfect for window boxes and hanging baskets—picture a blanket of yellow and orange nasturtiums tumbling from a second-story window box. Some annuals climb and can quickly cover a fence or trellis—imagine brilliant blue morning glories twining around your lamppost or framing your front door.

The oldest use of annuals is the traditional cutting garden. Because they bloom again and again, they can fill the house with the color and fragrance of cut flowers from spring through fall.

ANNUALS: OLD-FASHIONED FAVORITES

Annuals have been favorite flowers ever since history has been recorded. The ancient Greeks used carnations for garlands, and Napoleon regularly presented Josephine with mignonette and violets. Nowadays when we refer to old-fashioned flowers, we usually mean those that our grandmothers grew. Larkspur, pincushion flower, love-in-a-mist, cornflower, poppies, daisies, pinks and sweet peas are all beloved favorites. They were traditionally grown in cottage gardens of the colonists, and all were hardy annuals. It was some time later that tender annuals, such as petunias and zinnias from the tropics, became popular.

Many old-fashioned cottage favorites give pleasure to the nose as well as the eye. A walk at dusk when the air is permeated with perfume from your flower garden is a delight. Four-o'clocks open in the afternoon and release a rich, sweet scent; garden pinks have one of the sweetest smells; both the luxuriant flowers of stock and the ever-present sweet pea have charming fragrances and have graced our ancestors' gardens for generations.

Annual flowers may last for only a season, but their colors, scents and exuberant variety have given them a permanent place in gardens everywhere.

UNDERSTANDING FLOWERING PLANTS

ANNUAL, BIENNIAL OR PERENNIAL?

What is an annual? Very simply, a plant we call "annual" grows, flowers, produces seed and dies in one year. It completes its entire life or reproductive cycle between the last frosts of spring and the first frosts of autumn. In between, it must produce as many seeds as possible, for that is its function, and so it rewards even minimal care with a profusion of bloom.

Biennials have a two-year life cycle. In the first year, they grow only roots and foliage; in the second year, they bloom, produce seed and die.

A perennial, on the other hand, is a plant that lives from year to year. During the winter its leaves may die back, but its energy is stored in the roots and, come spring, it will send up new shoots to flower again.

Some perennials and biennials are treated, in gardens, as annuals—cultivated for one season only. These are plants that have been bred to bloom the first year. Pansies, forget-me-nots and statice are examples. Because we know you'll want to enjoy them, we've included some of these annual-like biennials and perennials on the following pages.

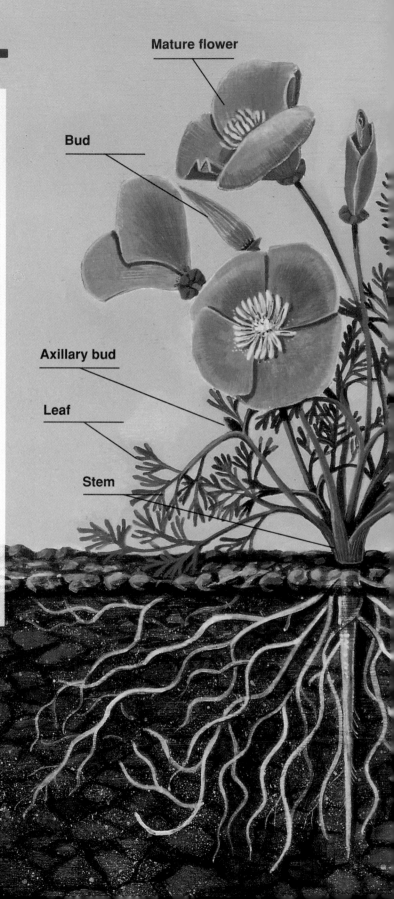

Mature flower

Bud

Axillary bud

Leaf

Stem

Magnified Flower Part

Stigma ⎤
Style   ⎬ **Pistil**
Ovary   ⎦

Anther   ⎤
Filament ⎬ **Stamen**

Spent flower

Seed pod

Root

HOW FLOWERS GROW

Despite its beauty and fragility, a flower is a very functional part of a plant. It produces the seeds so that new plants will grow and the species will survive.

Flowers have male and female parts for seed production. The male part, the *stamen*, consists of the *filament*—a slender stalk—and the *anther* at its top where pollen is made. The female part, the *pistil*, is made up of the *ovary*, where seeds are formed, and the *style*, a tube which leads upward from the ovary to the *stigma*, which receives the pollen. Pollen reaches the stigma by means of wind, insects or birds, and travels down the style to the ovary where seed formation begins. When mature, the seed pod will open and scatter the seeds to grow into new seedlings and complete the cycle.

Seedlings use sunlight and the chlorophyll in their leaves to combine water and nutrients from the soil with carbon dioxide from the air. This creates the food used by the plant to grow, flower and set seed.

Climate, amounts of sun and shade, water and soil composition all affect how well plants grow. Plants need a lot of nutrients which they take from the soil at a rapid rate. For plants to flourish, bloom and complete their life cycle, nutrients should be returned to the soil in the form of organic matter and fertilizers.

Six Flower Gardens

Annuals add color to almost every spot in the garden. They are used in formal or casual gardens, in cutting or fragrance gardens, in containers, in sun or shade. Here are six planting ideas to consider.

Containers are perfect for small gardens or to add lively color to the patio. See pgs. 18–19 for ideas on planting in containers and a list of commonly used plants.

Borders along a hedge, fence or wall provide for a continuous season of bloom. Annual vines can also form a cascade of flowers when entwined along a fence.

A cutting garden will fill the house with colorful flowers all summer long. Be sure to include a few taller plants, such as cosmos, zinnias, or tall marigolds. For a detailed list and care of cut flowers, see pgs. 20–21.

Use annuals to add accents to the perennial border. Low-growing annuals, such as sweet alyssum form attractive patterns along pathways.

Choose either one or two types of plants for best results in a mass bedding, such as impatiens, begonias, geraniums or petunias. Impatiens are excellent for shady areas.

Aromas will float through open windows and doors when a fragrance garden is planted nearby. Consider planting stock, sweet peas, or nicotiana, to name a few.

PLANNING YOUR GARDEN

Plantings of annuals can take many shapes and sizes. Gardens can consist entirely of annuals, or annuals can complement existing plantings—shrubs, trees and even vegetable plots. Flower groupings can be formal—laid out in rows or geometric shapes—or informal—in curved areas with plants in casual masses.

A bed or border of annuals can be large or small. It can curve along walks, driveways or the house's foundation, fill in areas between sidewalk and street, or soften walls or fences. A round or irregularly shaped island bed, surrounded by lawn, is another attractive design.

Bright annuals can dress up existing plantings. Intermixed with shrubs, annuals add color to a foundation planting. Added to a perennial border, they can enliven these gardens when some perennials are not blooming.

For small areas or spot planting, consider containers. On decks, patios, rooftops or poolside, annuals in tubs or pots can soften an expanse of wood or concrete. Maybe your garden is only a small city balcony; containers of flowering annuals can give it a country feeling. And don't forget hanging baskets and window boxes—both can add a charming accent to your home.

Another option is to plant a garden for cut flowers or fragrance alone. The cutting garden will consist of specific plants with long-lasting blooms and sturdy stems. A fragrance garden, confined to those plants with particularly sweet or spicy perfumes, can be a special treat. Plant it near a window, walkway or porch so you can enjoy the scents as you walk by or relax.

CHOOSING A SITE

Note the amount of sunlight and shade in each area where you plan to plant. Avoid dry, dark areas under low-branching shade trees. Plant shade-tolerant plants in open shaded areas with filtered sunlight.

Shrubs make a good background for colorful annuals.

An annual border looks great against a wall or fence.

Planting along the drive, a path or walkway creates a pleasant effect for you as well as passersby.

Climbing vines on a trellis create a striking vertical effect or screen.

Annuals in containers and window boxes add interest and make your home more inviting.

An island bed can create beauty to be seen from the patio as well as from the house.

Along the foundation of the house is an excellent place to add color. Be sure there is plenty of sun or part shade. Southern or eastern exposures are best.

WHERE TO PLANT

Prior to planting, determine the sunny and shady areas on your property. Note the amount of time each location gets sun and shade. Most annuals prefer full sun. Pick an area that gets six hours or more daily. For shaded areas, choose appropriate plants (see pgs. 22–23).

Also consider wind and heat. Soil in windy areas loses moisture more quickly and plants will need the protection of a windbreak, such as a wall or hedge. Extremely high temperatures in summer months can harm some annuals. Mulching helps to keep roots cool but, if you live in an area with consistently hot summers, choose heat tolerant annuals.

Avoid low spots that have poor drainage. Drainage is essential; the type of soil you have will determine the quality of drainage.

The best planned garden creates an attractive view both inside and outside the house. Choose areas you can see from the inside to enjoy the flowers fully. Areas outside of windows can be made to feel like an extension of that room. Plant around the outside sitting areas of the patio or terrace or along the front walkway. Don't neglect the walkway between the garage and the house. Since you use it every day, make it cheerful.

Always plan ahead and be realistic about the size of your garden. It's better to start small and be able to enjoy your garden than to take on too much. You can always add another area next season.

CHOOSING COLORS

Color creates the most immediate and enduring impression of a garden. From bright, bold colors to soothing cool ones, annuals provide a rainbow of colors for monochromatic schemes or bold, multicolored garden plans.

Celosia
Marigold
Nasturtium
Pansy
Portulaca
Sunflower

Yellows

Pinks

Begonia
Cosmos
Impatiens
Larkspur
Lavatera
Snapdragon
Sweet Pea

Reds

Amaranthus
Celosia
Geranium
Salvia
Sweet Pea
Sweet Sultan
Zinnia

Oranges

Calendula
Celosia
Marigold
Poppy
Snapdragon
Sunflower

Candytuft
Gypsophila
Moonflower
Sweet Alyssum
Sweet Pea
Vinca

Whites

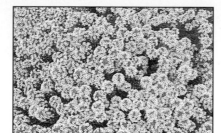

Blues

Ageratum
Bachelor's Button
Browallia
Forget-Me-Not
Larkspur
Morning Glory

Violets

Lobelia
Pansy
Petunia
Salpiglossis
Stock
Verbena

COMBINING COLORS

The color wheel is a useful guide for selecting color combinations for the garden. The warm tones—red, yellow and orange—draw your attention to them. Reds, for example, will seem closer to you than they really are. The cool colors—blue, violet and green—seem to recede. These subdued colors are best seen up close.

Complimentary colors—those opposite each other on the color wheel—produce good results when planted together. Orange and blue make a striking contrast; so do yellow and violet or red and green.

Analogous colors—those adjacent to each other on the color wheel—create harmony in the garden. Plant blues, blue-violet and violet together for a soft, cool effect.

Monochromatic gardens—those which use different flowers in shades of only one color—can be dramatic. An all-white border, for example, can be elegant and particularly beautiful at dusk.

Plant strong bold hues in a sunny garden and use pastels and whites to lighten up shady spots. Pastel pinks and mauves create a romantic feeling and look superb in front of dark shrubs or walls.

For best results, keep color schemes simple. Generous groups of each color have the best overall effect. Above all, let your own taste be your guide. Use your favorite shades, experiment and have fun!

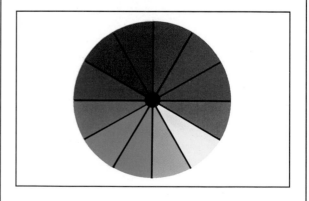

SPACE AND SIZE

There are three basic areas in the garden: the foreground, the middle and the background. Knowing the mature height and spread of the flowers you plant will help you in designing your garden.

Medium-sized plants from 1–2 1/2 ft. blend gradually and naturally to taller ones in back.

Low, compact or spreading plants from 4–12 in. make good edgings for the front of the border.

Use tall plants of 3–6 ft. to form the background plantings.

PLANT HEIGHT AND SPREAD

Once you've chosen the kind of garden you want, a location and a color scheme, it's time to make plant selections.

A major consideration is the size of the plant—both height and spread—when mature. You want to avoid overcrowding and make sure some plants don't cast shadows on others, reducing sunlight. At the same time, it's desirable for the garden to look full, without a lot of bare ground between plants. (See Plant Data Chart, pgs. 74–77.)

Divide the flower bed or border roughly into background, middle and foreground sections. Use the tallest plants for the back. Tall annuals, such as cleome or cosmos, will provide a backdrop for the flowers in front.

The middle section will contain most of your flowers. Medium and medium-tall plants—from which there are many to choose—will create a natural cascade from the back to the front of the garden.

Place low-growing, edging plants in the foreground. Alyssum, ageratum or lobelia are some that set off, but do not shield, the plants behind.

If you plan an island bed to be viewed from all sides, the tallest plants belong in the center, surrounded by medium-sized plants. Place compact plants around the outside rim.

Consider plant foliage, too—a variety of leaf color and textures can add interest to the garden. Cosmos, for example, has delicate fernlike foliage. The silvery leaves of dusty miller can highlight other garden colors. Coleus is best known for its colorful foliage and can also be brought indoors as a winter house plant.

COLORFUL CONTAINERS

Plants for Containers

Ageratum	Nasturtium
Alyssum	Pansy
Browallia	Petunia
Dusty Miller	Thunbergia
Geranium	Verbena
Lobelia	Vinca
Impatiens	Zinnia
Marigold	

Planting in Containers

First Select a decorative container with adequate drainage. Fill with sterilized potting soil.

Next Mix in slow-release fertilizer at label rate. Fertilize every 2 weeks with a water-soluble fertilizer.

Last Select plants that are varied in height and complementary in color. Plant close together. Water thoroughly.

Hanging Baskets

First Line a wire basket with a 1–1 1/2 in. thick layer of sphagnum moss that has been soaked in water.

Next Fill basket to 1 in. from the top with 3/4 potting soil and 1/4 peat moss mix. Sprinkle slow-release fertilizer at label rate.

Last Select full or trailing plants for best display and plant close together. Water thoroughly.

ANNUALS IN CONTAINERS

Annuals are the plants of choice for containers. Their long bloom time, exquisite display of color and low maintenance make them naturals for pots, window boxes and hanging baskets. You need only to water well, fertilize regularly and pinch off the faded blooms to have color all season.

Choose a variety of containers—clay or plastic pots, urns, aged whiskey barrels, buckets or even an old wheelbarrow. Just about anything that holds soil will do. If you are grouping an arrangement on a wall or the terrace, buy an assortment of shapes in roughly the same size for the best effect. Large containers will hold more soil which will mean less watering and more room for combinations of plants.

Good drainage is essential. Make sure your containers have a drainage hole. Use sterilized potting soil. Soil directly from your garden may contain weed seeds, pests or fungi; it also will not drain as well as commercially prepared soil. Commercial soil is also lighter in weight, which is preferred for hanging plants.

When choosing annuals for your containers, choose flowers with the longest bloom time and plants that do not need staking. For hanging baskets choose those with a trailing habit.

Plants in containers are exposed to the elements more readily than plants in the ground and will need watering more frequently. In hot summer months this may mean daily. Due to frequent waterings, essential nutrients are leached through the soil. Fertilize regularly with a water soluble fertilizer. Remove faded blooms continually and check for insects on a regular basis. These simple tips will provide you with colorful plants all summer and into the fall.

CAUTION

Soil from your garden could contain weed seed, pests or a disease. Use sterilized potting soil for best results.

19

Cut Flowers

Annuals lend luxuriant color and delightful fragrance to the garden and to every room in the house. The best cutting annuals have long-lasting flowers and sturdy stems. Plant enough of each so cutting won't deplete the garden.

Annuals for Cutting

Aster	Marigold
Blue Lace Flower	Mignonette
Calendula	Poppy
Candytuft	Prairie Gentian
Celosia	Salpiglossis
Clarkia	Scabiosa
Cosmos	Snapdragon
Dianthus	Stock
Gaillardia	Sunflower
Globe Amaranth	Sweet Pea
Gloriosa Daisy	Sweet Sultan
Gypsophila	Verbena
Heliotrope	Zinnia
Larkspur	

CARE OF CUT FLOWERS

Careful cutting and handling of fresh flowers can extend the life of your cut flower bouquets.

Select open or partially open blooms and cut them in the cool of early morning or evening; flowers wilt faster in midday heat. Bring a pail of water with you into the garden and submerge cut stems immediately.

Using a sharp knife or hand shears, cut stems at a 45-degree angle, for maximum water intake. Other types of scissors can damage stems.

Bring cut flowers indoors or to a cool shaded area. Remove all leaves that fall below the water line. Cutting stems again, underwater, will further increase water uptake and lengthen vase life. Remove flowers from pail and place in a solution of warm water and floral preservative in the vase of your choice. Dahlias, poppies and snow-on-the-mountain leak milky sap when cut. Before putting these flowers in the vase, sear cut stem ends with a lighted match.

Floral preservatives prolong the freshness of cut flowers. They contain sugar, a bactericide/fungicide and an acidifer. These ingredients feed the plant and inhibit the growth of bacteria which can clog stems. Preservatives are available at nurseries, hardware and grocery stores or by mail. You can mix a batch and store it, labeled and covered, in a cool place for several days to use as needed.

SHADE ANNUALS

ANNUALS FOR SHADE

While many annuals prefer sun most of the day to perform well, by choosing plants wisely, you can have color in those shady areas by a wall, on a porch, on the north side of the house and under trees.

Annuals for Light Shade

Alyssum	Phlox
Clarkia	Pansy
Cleome	Snapdragon
Coleus	Sweet Sultan
Nasturtium	

Annuals for Medium or Partial Shade

Begonia	Lobelia
Browallia	Monkey Flower
Canterbury Bells	Nicotiana
Celosia	Salvia
Coleus	Stock
Forget-Me-Not	Thunbergia
Foxglove	Vinca
Impatiens	Wishbone Flower

Annuals for Deep Shade

Coleus	Impatiens

COLOR IN THE SHADE

Seed packets and nursery tags describe shade as "light," "medium" or "partial" and "deep." Before choosing plants for specific areas of your garden, consider the amount of sunlight each area receives daily.

An area of light shade is one in shadow three to four hours per day. Medium or partial shade areas are without sun for four to six hours—these are usually places that receive only morning or afternoon sun. Deep shade describes those areas that get little or no sun.

In light to medium shade areas, many annuals will bloom and be healthy. Nasturtiums, pansies and clarkia all flower well in light shade conditions. Wax begonia puts forth its many-colored blooms continuously in shaded beds, borders or containers. Browallia's cascading habit and profuse lavender blossoms can make a charming hanging basket on a shady porch.

Under trees, shade may be dappled, with sunlight filtering through loose foliage. In these areas, use plants designated for medium shade. Other trees, because of dense or low-growing foliage and branches, create a deep-shade environment under their limbs. There you will have success with impatiens, which flowers continuously in many colors, or coleus with its richly colored foliage. If possible, trim branches to let more light in.

Beds along west-facing walls can get very hot on summer afternoons even though they are in the sun for only half the day. Choose full sun annuals for these locations.

STARTING ANNUALS FROM SEED

INDOOR SOWING FOR EARLY BLOOMS

Starting seeds indoors will give you earlier blooms in the garden and extends the growing season in cool-climate areas.

Starting seeds is not complicated. All you need is a clean container, which you can buy or make, a sterile seed-starting soil mix, light, water and seed.

Check seed packets for instructions on when to plant. You want to start seeds indoors at least four to eight weeks before the last frost date in your location. Make sure your container has drainage holes in the bottom. Then fill the container with sterile seed-starting soil mix, not garden soil which can contain diseases. Place the container on a tray and water until soil is moist throughout.

Plant seeds at the depth the package indicates. Plant more seeds than you will need, so you can select the strongest seedlings. After planting, spray soil lightly with water from a fine mist spray bottle. Label the flat with plant names.

Loosely cover the entire container with plastic wrap. Be sure to punch a few holes in the wrap to allow ventilation. There are also commercially available flats with plastic covers at garden centers. Do not water the soil unless dry at the surface.

When seeds sprout, remove the wrap and place container in a window where it will receive full sun. When first true leaves appear, you can begin to fertilize the seedlings. Feed weekly with a liquid plant fertilizer at 1/4 strength, following package directions.

Starting Seeds Indoors

First Fill flat container with sterilized potting soil and soak thoroughly.

Fourth Clearly label plants and cover with plastic wrap or cover to keep moisture in.

Then Sow seeds and firm soil. Sow more seeds than you think you'll need.

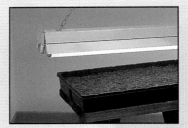

Next Put container in a warm, bright location or under a household fluorescent bulb 24 hrs. per day until seeds sprout.

Third Water gently with spray bottle; water should be at room temperature. Take care not to over-water or let container sit in water.

Last Remove plastic when seeds sprout. Make sure soil is moist, not wet. When first true leaves appear, fertilize with 1/4 strength liquid fertilizer. Feed weekly.

GROWING SEEDLINGS

HEALTHY SEEDLINGS

Healthy seedlings are a rich green, have sturdy stems and are compact, not tall or spindly. Following a few simple guidelines will keep your seedlings healthy.

Purchase potting mix or sterile soil from your garden center. Soil from the garden will drain poorly in a container and may contain pests and diseases. Keep the soil moist, not wet; over-watering can literally drown a plant, robbing it of oxygen. Make sure the plants have enough light. In a window, they need full-day sun. Under fluorescent bulbs, they need 12-14 hours of light daily, with the bulb placed six inches from the top of plants.

When the second set of true leaves appears, seedlings are ready to be transplanted. Select the strongest ones and discard the rest. Transplant each plant to its own small pot or cell.

Partially fill individual cells or pots with soil. Moisten soil. Lift seedling from the flat with a wooden stick or spoon, leaving as much soil on the roots as possible. Place the seedling gently in the new pot, and add more soil to just below the bottom leaves. Firm soil around the seedling so that it stands upright. Add more soil if needed. Water the soil gently.

Do not over-water young plants, and give them plenty of light daily. In a window, rotate them periodically so they don't lean toward the light. Feed young plants with 1/4 strength liquid fertilizer once a week.

Always *harden off* (see pgs. 34-35) your home grown bedding plants prior to planting outside by putting them in a coldframe or placing them outside for limited amounts of time each day. When they are hardened off, transplant them to the garden.

Transplanting Seedlings

First Remove seedlings from flat with flat wooden stick or spoon. Hold seedling by leaf—not stem.

Next Plant each seedling in an individual cell with leaves just above the new soil line. Firm soil around plant. Water gently. Keep soil moist, but do not over-water.

Last When first true leaves appear, fertilize once a week with 1/4 strength 10–10–10 or 10–5–5 fertilizer.

Seedling Problems and Solutions

HEALTHY SEEDLINGS

Note the compact growth of leaves and strong, erect stems on this healthy seedling. With proper light and watering your seedlings will not become too tall or leggy. The leaves will be a rich green color with no yellowing.

LEGGY AND SCRAWNY SEEDLINGS

Problem: Plant stem is thin and seems to stretch. Seedling is tall with few leaves, spindly.

Solution: Provide more light. Seedlings need full-day sun or 12–14 hrs. of fluorescent light per day. Also, keep plants moist, not wet.

DAMPING OFF

Problem: Seedling fallen over; it appears pinched at the base.

Solution: Use sterilized soil. If using equipment from last year, clean with a solution of 10 drops of bleach to one gallon of water. Damping off is caused by a fungus; you can also prevent its spread by providing sun and good air circulation.

YELLOW SEEDLINGS

Problem: Seedling is pale green or yellowing, possibly from overwatering.

Solution: Fertilize adequately to provide needed nutrients. Apply 1/4 strength liquid fertilizer, following package directions. Do not over-fertilize.

SELECTING
VIGOROUS PLANTS

Labels should be clear. Look for improved varieties or hybrids; these are usually bred for more blooms and are more vigorous.

Healthy, firm and even top growth and no signs of injury.

Purchase plants with good bud development but not too many flowers.

ULTRA ROSE

PETUNIA

Leaf color should be green with no blemished or yellow leaves.

Stems should be sturdy and compact, not weak or leggy.

Look under leaves for pests or signs of stress and disease.

Make sure the soil is moist, not dry and crumbling.

Roots should not be growing through the drainage holes.

CHOOSING BEDDING PLANTS

If you do not wish to grow annuals from seed, you can purchase ready-to-transplant annuals from the garden center or nursery. Bedding plants come in four, six, or jumbo packs, two and four inch pots or flats.

Although it is more expensive to purchase these transplants, there are several advantages. If you do not have the time or space to devote to starting seeds indoors, you may purchase plants after the soil has warmed and plant them in late spring or early summer; you can see exactly what you are buying, inspect it on the spot and take it home. Plants from the garden center are usually starting to bloom; seeing actual flowers makes it easy to define your color scheme.

It is best to prepare the soil in your garden prior to purchasing plants at the nursery (see pgs. 32–33). If you have to purchase your plants before you are ready to transplant, put them in a cool, shaded place and keep them moist.

Always purchase plants that are carefully labeled. Do not purchase unnamed, poor grade stock. Plants rarely recover from a poor start in life. Check over your plants carefully using the guidelines on the left.

Do not expect your nursery to carry all of the varieties listed in this book. Most garden centers are limited by space, and many specialize in certain types of annuals. For more varieties at much less cost, start your own seeds.

IDEAL SOIL

SOIL AND PLANTS

Most garden soils are mixtures of clay, silt, and sand. Clay drains poorly; sand dries out quickly. The best soils are loams containing sand, silt, clay, and organic matter. These soils are easy to work and hold water and air.

Good soil structure makes a world of difference in how well your plants grow. If your soil is too packed, there isn't enough pore space for air to penetrate and the soil can't draw water up and down to feed root systems. Surface water runs off without penetrating and plant roots grow weak and shallow. If your soil structure is too grainy, nutrients will penetrate quickly but won't stay long enough for roots to use them.

Poor drainage is also a major cause of plant problems. If your water table is too high or your garden has poor drainage, your plants will be vulnerable to root rot, toxic salt buildup and shallow root structures that cause plants to wilt rapidly in dry spells. With poor drainage harmful parasites will flourish but earthworms won't, and little oxygen will reach your plants' roots.

Annuals which will tolerate poor soil include: alyssum, balsam, celosia, cleome, four-o'clock, gaillardia, nasturtium, California poppy, petunia, portulaca and sweet sultan.

TYPES OF SOIL

CLAY SOIL Clay soil is made up of very tiny flat inorganic particles that become easily compacted and hard. It is often called "heavy" soil because it packs together densely, holding water and impairing drainage. Wet clay is sticky and holds firm. Dry clay is hard. Compost is an excellent conditioner to add to clay soil.

SANDY SOIL Sandy soil features large individual mineral particles and a lot of air space. It crumbles easily when squeezed. Often called "light" soil, it permits roots to penetrate readily, but allows water and nutrients to drain away quickly. Compost and peat moss are both good amendments to add to sandy soil.

SILT SOIL Silt has small sized mineral particles that are larger than clay and smaller than sand. Dry silt, when squeezed, breaks up and is lumpy. It retains water well but lacks important air space between particles.

LOAM SOIL Often called the ideal soil, loam contains nearly equal parts of clay, silt, sand and organic matter. It retains moisture, air and nutrients yet drains easily. It's also referred to as "loose" or "friable" soil.

IDEAL SOIL FOR ANNUALS

Annuals do best in loam that drains well, is slightly acidic, as opposed to alkaline, and is rich in nutrients.

A simple test will show you the composition of your soil by how well it drains. Dig a hole one foot across and one foot deep in soil that has not been irrigated for several days. Fill the hole with water. Time how long it takes for the water to soak in completely.

If the water drains in less than five minutes, your soil is sandy. If it takes more than 15 minutes to drain, your soil is mostly clay. Both can be improved by adding organic matter (see pg. 33).

To determine whether your soil is acidic or alkaline, have a sample professionally tested by your county Agricultural Extension Service, or test it yourself with one of the many kits available in garden centers. A pH reading of 6.5—slightly acid—is best for annuals.

If your soil proves too acidic, you will need to add lime. Alkaline soil can be neutralized by adding sulfur or gypsum.

Prepare flower beds just before planting. Whenever your garden soil becomes compacted, or depleted of basic nutrients, you need to renovate the flower bed.

Preparing to Plant

After choosing the location for your annuals you are ready to begin digging and preparing your soil. For small areas, double-digging is the best method. For large areas, use a rotary tiller to turn over your soil. It's best to till twice in order to loosen the soil deep enough for good root development.

Double-Digging

First Outline area with garden lime or flour.

Then Cut and roll grass for disposal if bed is in existing lawn.

Third Remove 8–10 in. of soil off to the side of the bed.

Fourth Use a pitchfork to loosen subsoil another 8–10 in.

Next Add 4–6 in. of organic amendments to the subsoil and mix.

Last Return topsoil mixed with more amendments and fertilizer; rake and level.

SOIL AMENDMENTS

Rarely does an undeveloped garden have ideal soil; therefore, amendments are needed to adjust your soil. Once you have determined what kind of soil you have, you will know what to look for in an amendment.

If your soil has too much clay or sand, you should add organic matter such as compost, leaf mold or well-rotted manure. These and other organic materials may be purchased at your local nursery. If you don't have a compost pile, it's a good idea to start one; compost is an excellent soil conditioner. You can also use lightweight amendments, such as vermiculite or perlite.

Adding organic matter improves the texture of the soil and greatly improves drainage. Heavy clay soil will be opened up and lighter. Sandy soil needs organic matter to retain moisture and nutrients normally leached quickly through the sand. For annuals, 30 percent of the total soil volume for your bed should be organic matter. The soil color will be a darker, richer brown. Add organic matter yearly.

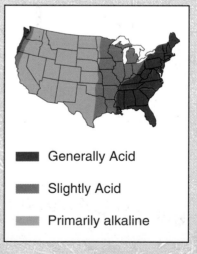

■ Generally Acid

■ Slightly Acid

■ Primarily alkaline

TRANSPLANTING OUTDOORS

PLANTING TRANSPLANTS

Seedlings grown in an indoor environment have to get used to an outdoor environment slowly. If you put them directly in the garden from the protection of your home, you could damage them. Before they can be planted in the garden, seedlings need to be *hardened off*. Hardening off is the process of exposing plants gradually to outdoor conditions. Put plants in a cold frame or on a screened porch for a few hours each day, lengthening the time each day. Keep them in the shade for the first two days and gradually move them into the sun. After several days, you should see signs of leaf growth and stems becoming stronger. In about a week, they should be ready for transplanting. This period of acclimation is necessary for all annuals, especially tender annuals.

Prepare your garden site beforehand and have it ready to receive transplants if possible. Choose a cloudy day with no wind. For continually sunny areas, transplant in early morning or late afternoon. To avoid the hot sun, create shade by covering seedlings with a lath or cheesecloth. Water the transplants before planting to make the rootball easier to remove. Note the spread of each plant at its maturity and space far enough apart so that each plant can grow without crowding its neighbor. Place seedlings at the same soil depth as they were in pots, being careful not to bury leaves.

Transplanting Annuals

First When plants have 3–4 sets of leaves, harden outdoors in a coldframe or on a screen porch by exposing gradually to outdoor conditions.

Fourth If soil feels crumbly as the plant is removed, use a dull knife or trowel to retain as much soil as possible around the roots.

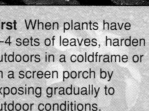

Then Use a trowel to make hole deep and wide enough to place plant.

Next Press soil firmly around plant and water gently but thoroughly.

Third Water plants and allow to drain well for easier removal. Remove plant from container by pressing on the sides and the bottom. Ease plant out.

Last If sun is intense, protect seedling by creating shade with a lath or cheesecloth.

WATERING

THE IMPORTANCE OF WATER

Water is essential for your annuals to grow and flourish. Plants grow quickly with a steady supply but wilt and show other signs of stress with too little or too erratic a supply. Even drought-tolerant varieties need a regular supply; they just don't need to be watered as often.

A common mistake among beginning gardeners is to under-water. Knowing when to water means recognizing a few important signs. The most important is wilting: do not let your plants get to the wilting stage before you water them—check soil surface and slightly below for dryness often. After you have transplanted a seedling, water it right away to prevent wilting. You can "muddy in" plants that are set widely apart, that is, water so thoroughly that a mud puddle forms around each plant.

Too much water can also stress your plants. If you have heavy or clay soil, the top may seem dry, while moisture is just below the surface. When the ground becomes saturated, plants may develop disease or drown because air cannot reach the roots. Soil that is wet for a prolonged period can actually rot plants' roots. Consequently, good soil drainage is essential.

CHECKING IF WATER IS NEEDED Here's a simple test: Use a trowel to dig into the soil, about 8–10 in. away from your plants. For transplants, the layer of dry soil should not be more than 1/2 in. deep; for established plants, more than 1–2 in. of dry soil means it's time to water deeply.

ROOT LEVEL WATERING: Root level watering is the most efficient use of water. This is done by hand or bubble hose at the base of the plant. Give 1–2 in. of water. After soaking in, the ground should be moist at least 6 in. down and should stay wet 3–5 days barring a heat spell.

WHEN TO WATER

How much and how often you water your annuals depends on your soil type and climate. Clay soils hold more water. Sandy soils dry out quickly. If you live in a hot, dry area, you will have to water more. Wind also robs moisture from plants. Cool areas can have extended heat spells, which are hard on tender plants. Use common sense when watering and follow a few simple guidelines.

When seeds are sown directly into the garden, they must be watered daily until they germinate. Once sprouted, seedlings should be watered every other day, more if soil dries out.

Established plants need an average of one inch of water per week. A deep soaking is better than several light sprinklings to develop root growth.

To determine if plants need water, dig down to one to two inches below the soil surface. If soil is still dry at that depth, water. Remember, young plants have shallow root systems. Water them when soil is dry one-half inch down.

Different watering devices deliver different amounts of water per hour. Using a rain gauge is the best way to know if you—or Mother Nature—have applied the required one inch of irrigation.

FERTILIZING

Most annuals bloom well without fertilizer. However, even a single application will make for larger, vigorous plants, often with many more blooms. There are some annuals, such as begonias, geraniums and petunias, that are heavy feeders and require regular fertilizing for continuous bloom.

Dry Organics

First Transport well-rotted, not fresh, manure directly to site.

Then Use hand cultivator to work in below surface to reach roots quickly.

Dry Synthetics

First All-purpose fertilizers are easy to apply but measure carefully. Injury may occur if you over-apply.

Then Sprinkle around plant and work in well.

Liquid or Mixed Powders

First Liquids like fish emulsion must be mixed or diluted according to label.

Then Apply evenly around the base of the plant.

CHOOSING FERTILIZERS

Fertilizers come in either organic or synthetic forms. Organic fertilizers, sometimes called *natural organics*, are those that occur naturally from plants or animals. Examples are manure, bone meal and fish emulsion. Synthetic or chemically processed fertilizers include superphosphate, ammonium sulfate and sulfate of potash. They have the advantages of premixed proportions, compact storage and low cost. However, use with caution—they may burn plants. The advantage of using some organics is that they contribute to the soil structure, improving water- and nutrient-holding capability.

Blooming annuals generally use a 5-10-10 proportion of nitrogen-phosphorus-potassium. Phosphorous is *the* most important ingredient for flowering annuals, as it promotes flowering and subsequent seed production. Bone meal is the most common natural source of phosphorus. Once mature, annuals need the lowest percentage of nitrogen, which promotes leaf growth sometimes at the expense of flowers.

Each fertilizer contains a different amount and proportion of nutrients. Read the label to see how much N-P-K (nitrogen-phosphorus-potassium) it contains. The N-P-K number (10-10-10) represents the percentage by weight of each ingredient. The label also shows the amount of fertilizer to apply. Examine the nutrient balance of organics carefully—you may have to supplement with synthetics.

Foliar Fertilizers

First Dilute or mix foliar fertilizers in watering can or directly in the container to be attached to the hose.

Then Spray evenly onto the leaves at the recommended rate.

IN-SEASON CARE

Although annuals require minimum maintenance, there are a few things you can do to make bushier plants or keep plants blooming longer.

40

Applying Mulch

First Spread mulch 1–2 in. deep around bedding area. Mulch will conserve moisture, maintain a steady soil temperature and cut down on weeds.

Last Be sure to keep mulch 3–4 in. away from the base of each plant.

Pinching Back Pinching back new growth will force branching, creating bushier plants. Pinch off the top point of the stem down to mature leaves.

Deadheading Deadheading or cutting off faded blossoms stops seed production and promotes flowering. It also keeps the plant more attractive.

Staking Staking plants will keep tall, blooming plants from falling over. Stake plants when small. Tie plants loosely and add more ties as plants grow.

WEEDING

WEED CONTROL

The best way to control weeds is to stay ahead of them. Mulch will keep most weeds away. If you are not using mulch, pull weeds while they are small, before they set seed.

Weeds are harmful. They compete with your annuals for nutrients and water as well as crowd and shade the plants. They also can harbor pests and diseases.

Methods of controlling weeds vary. The old-fashioned way, and probably still the best, is to pull them by hand. If you catch them before they have established long root systems, this is fairly simple. Use a hoe, cultivator or trowel after weeds are established to ensure you take out as much root as possible. Some weeds, like dandelions, have long taproots. A long-handled, pronged dandelion cutter is good for all tap-rooted weeds. Always keep a tool nearby when weeding. When a weed doesn't pull up easily, dig in the trowel to loosen the roots, and then pull the weed. Take care not to disturb the nearby plants.

Mulching can help contain the growth of weeds. Very few weeds are able to grow through a cover of pine bark, wood chips, or other mulching material. Those that do pop up are easy to pull. Mulch also conserves moisture and keeps the soil temperature cool.

The easiest time to weed is after a rain when the soil is moist. Moist soil is more pliable and allows you to pull the entire root out.

Bindweed
Convolvulus arvensis
A deep-rooted perennial vine that twines itself around the stems of a host plant. Flowers are pink or white. Smothers plants. Must be dug up.

Chickweed
Stellaria media
A prolific seed-producer that's easy to eradicate, but do so at first sign. An annual, it grows in any soil and has small, white, star-shaped flowers. Use cultivator to cut off just below soil line.

Crabgrass
Digitaria sanguinalis
An annual grass that spreads flat from the center and is almost impossible to get a hold of without a tool. Grows in any soil. Must be dug out.

Dandelion
Taraxacum officinale
This common weed grows in most of the world. It's yellow flower has a very long taproot that must be dug out. Remove before it goes to seed.

Purslane
Portulaca oleracea
A smaller, rounder version of the flowering garden variety. Heat tolerant. Spreads rapidly by seed, so pull at first sign. Regenerates if any root is left behind.

Quackgrass
Agropyron repens
A prolific perennial weed. Spreads rapidly by underground stolons or by seeds. Remove early, before seeds set, and carefully, as every piece will regenerate a new plant.

PESTS AND DISEASES

Aster yellows virus affects asters and also marigolds and other annuals. Plants are stunted and yellow. Flowers are yellow and sometimes green. Remove and destroy infected plants.

Aphids are small piercing insects that suck plant juices from the stem and leaves and spread disease. Ladybugs eat them. Insecticidal soap also discourages them.

Aphid

Slugs and snails are common and extremely destructive night-feeding pests. A ring of wood ashes or sharp sand around each plant keeps them away.

Powdery mildew is a white fungus growth on the leaves and stems. Badly infected plants can die. Crowded or wet plants encourage the growth.

Snail

Slug

Mealy bugs are white insects that pierce and suck plant juices. Groups cluster in cottony masses. Insecticidal soap eliminates the bugs.

Mealybug

Cutworms stay buried in the soil by day and come out by night to chew on plant stems. Plant collars work fairly well to keep them at bay.

CONTROL METHODS

Annuals are hindered by relatively few pests and diseases. There are occasions, however, where trouble can strike.

The best pest and disease control is prevention. Keeping your garden clean, removing weeds and watering early in the day are sound preventive measures. Choosing disease-resistant varieties is also helpful. Providing a good soil structure will promote more vigorous plants.

Examine your plants to detect early signs of pests and diseases. Waiting until the damage is done is oftentimes too late. Learn to recognize pests and diseases and their symptoms. At the first sign, act immediately. Waiting for even a day can be too late. Use control measures designed for the specific problem at hand.

Insects are usually the biggest problem. Learn to identify the "bad" insects from the "good" insects and pests. Aphids, mealybugs, slugs and snails all do damage. Ladybugs, preying mantises and green lacewings are all beneficial insects that feed on pests and their eggs and larvae. Ladybugs will devour aphids as will the green lacewing. Birds and toads will also eat pests. A single house wren can eat up to 1,000 insects a day, while the toad not only eats insects but also slugs.

If you keep your garden clean and use biological controls, you should have no need for chemical controls. This is especially true for annuals, as they are around for only one growing season.

45

ANNUAL PLANT GALLERY

The following pages feature many of the most popular annuals. They are listed in alphabetical order by common name, followed by biological name or species.

African Daisy
Dimorphotheca hybrids

Also known as Cape marigold, the African daisy grows to 1 ft. tall and has profuse 3 in. daisy-like flowers in apricot, pink, orange and yellow, usually with dark centers. Blooms in summer and fall, or winter and spring in warm winter areas. Plant in full sun and well-drained soil; excellent for hot, dry areas. Flowers close on cloudy days and at night.

Ageratum
Ageratum houstonianum

One of the most popular edging plants, 6–12 in. tall, ageratum has clusters of fuzzy flowers in delicate blue and lavender shades. Blooms in summer and fall. Use in masses along beds, borders, walks or in containers. Tolerates light shade.

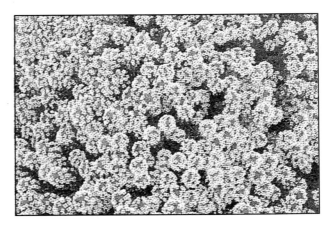

Alyssum, Sweet
Lobularia maritima

Low-growing plants 4–6 in. tall with clusters of tiny fragrant white flowers, sweet alyssum is excellent for edging or container plantings. It prefers sun or light shade. Sow directly in the garden as soon as soil is workable in the spring. Cut back to improve untidy plants.

Alyssum, Sweet Purple

Lobularia maritima

Sweet alyssum doesn't have to be white. Varieties now include lavender, pink, and violet. All are easy to grow from seed, blooming in 6 weeks. These plants are perfect as border plants, among perennials or bulbs and in hanging baskets. All sweet alyssum reseed freely.

Balsam

Impatiens balsamina

A Victorian favorite, balsam grows 1–3 ft. tall . Most bear double or semi-double blooms during summer and fall in various colors resembling small camellias. For best results, plant in sun or partial shade in rich, moist soil. Keep moist and well fed. Long flowering. Reseeds easily.

Amaranthus

Amaranthus tricolor

Also called Joseph's coat, amaranthus is a bold, striking plant. It grows 3–5 ft. tall and has tricolored leaves of bright red, yellow and green. Sow directly into the garden when soil is warm. Tolerates heat. Love-lies-bleeding or *A. caudatus* is another species with long, drooping red flowers and red leaves.

Bachelor's Button

Centaurea cyanus

Also called cornflower, this is one of the prettiest blue flowers in the garden. The plant is very hardy, growing 1–3 ft. tall. Flowers can also be red, pink or white; some are double. Sow directly in cool soil outdoors, as bachelor's button does not transplant well. Plant successively for additional blooms. Excellent cut flower.

ANNUAL PLANT GALLERY

Begonia, Wax
Begonia semperflorens

Wax begonia is one of the most popular of all garden plants. Its nonstop displays come in red, pink and white flowers with bronze or green foliage; some have double flowers. Just 6–12 in. tall, the begonia is excellent for window boxes, beds and borders. Easy to grow in rich, moist soil, in shade or sun. While it is readily available in nurseries, some selections are available only in seed. Blooms year round in Zones 9–10.

Bells of Ireland
Moluccella laevis

A tall, spiked plant of chartreuse bells that grows 18 in. tall, bells of Ireland makes an interesting and unusual addition to the middle or back of a border. Plant in sun or light shade and keep moist. Blooms in summer and fall. Reseeds readily. Flowers may be dried.

Browallia
Browallia speciosa

An excellent choice for the shade, this low-growing plant is commonly in blue and purple hues. It grows 12–15 in. high and trails well, making it a prime choice for hanging baskets. Plant in rich, well-drained soil. Trim plants back and bring inside before fall frosts for winter blooms.

Butterfly Flower
Schizanthus pinnatus

A combination of small orchid-like flowers and delicate fern-like foliage make the butterfly flower a valuable annual for containers or semi-shady spots. This small 1 ft. plant is covered with pink, rose, lilac, purple, white or red flowers all showing off yellow throats. Filtered shade, moist soil and ample water are best for success.

California Poppy
Eschscholzia californica

This state flower of California is easy to grow with spectacular results. Reaching 1 ft. in height, it produces vivid yellow, pink, orange or white flowers in spring and summer. It is striking massed in borders or in a wildflower garden and may be perennial in some areas. Plant directly into the soil in full sun.

Calendula
Calendula officinalis

Commonly called pot marigold, this is one of the easiest annuals to grow and the most prolific, bearing numerous large double yellow and orange blooms in the spring through the fall. The plant will reach 2 ft. tall. It tolerates any soil and all conditions except deep shade or intense heat. Sow a second planting in mid-summer for great fall color. It is one of the best annuals for winter color in warm regions. Good cut flower.

Candytuft
Iberis umbellata

Candytuft is a compact, low-growing annual that forms dense mats of showy flowers in clusters. Blooms grow on erect stems 8–14 in. tall and come in an array of pastel colors. Sow directly in full sun. Fall-sown seeds in Zones 8–10 will produce winter blooms. Good addition to a fragrance garden.

ANNUAL PLANT GALLERY

Celosia, Crested
Celosia cristata

Often called cockscomb, this velvety flower resembles the head of a rooster. It is available in dwarf and tall varieties and flowers come in a multitude of colors. Sow directly into the garden in full sun, and it will bloom from mid-summer to frost. Excellent for cutting and drying.

Celosia, Plumed
Celosia plumosa

Resembling a feather plume or a flame, the flowers on this showy celosia come in reds, yellows, oranges and pinks. Reliable and easy to grow, the plant will reach 2–3 ft. Dwarf varieties, good for edging, are also available. Sow directly into the garden in full sun and almost any soil. Tolerates heat.

Carnation
Dianthus caryophyllus

Carnation flowers produce one of the loveliest spicy scents in the garden. Some varieties can grow to 2 ft.; new, compact varieties grow to only 12 in. tall and produce many double flowers in a multitude of colors and bicolors. All have attractive blue-green leaves. Plant in full sun and warm soil, or indoors for earlier bloom. Newer varieties are heat resistant; taller ones make good cut flowers. It may be a short-lived perennial in mild climates.

Chrysanthemum
Chrysanthemum paludosum

Looking like miniature Shasta daisies, these tiny white flowers form on a dwarf, bushy plant that reaches 10 in. tall. With gray-green toothed leaves and plenty of flowers, this paludosum daisy likes full sun and does well in beds, borders and pots.

Coleus
Coleus x hybridus

Grown for its colorful foliage, coleus comes in a kaleidoscope of leaf colors and patterns. It grows to 1 ft. tall and thrives in the shade. It shows well in pots and baskets. Blooms from the spring into the fall. Pinch flowers off to keep compact. Bring indoors for the winter as house plants.

Cleome
Cleome hasslerana

A dramatic, tall plant, cleome grows quickly to 3–6 ft. Round white, pink or lavender flower heads with long stamens give it a spidery look, hence its common name of spider flower. Plant in sun or light shade in most any soil. Cleome produces abundant flowers from early summer to frost and is particularly effective at the back of a border or along a wall or fence.

Cosmos
Cosmos bipinnatus

Cosmos has charming daisy-like blooms in rose, pink and white and distinctive feathery foliage. It grows rapidly to 5 ft. tall and blooms in summer and fall. Plant in full sun. *Cosmos sulphureus* is more compact with yellow or orange blooms. Dwarf varieties grow to 1 ft. Excellent cut flower.

ANNUAL PLANT GALLERY

Dahlia
Dahlia species

Available in an array of bright colors, dahlias bloom freely until frost. Plant in sun or light shade and feed and water regularly. Pinch side buds for larger blooms. Excellent cut flower and bedding plant. For best results, keep bed mulched.

Dahlberg Daisy
Dyssodia tenuiloba

Few plants can outlast this gem of low-growing (4–6 in.) golden, daisy-like flowers that bloom from early summer to frost against a dark green background of finely divided, thread-like leaves. Plant in full sun; it tolerates less water than most annuals. Prolific bloom and fine foliage make it a stunning groundcover. It may become perennial in mild-winter areas. Reseeds.

Dianthus
Dianthus chinensis

Also known as pinks, dianthus is an old-fashioned favorite for beds, borders, edging and containers. Bushy and compact, it grows to 12 in. high. Flowers are pink, white, coral, red and bicolored against blue-gray leaves. Dianthus does well in full sun or light shade, tolerates poor soils and will self-sow if surrounding soil is undisturbed.

Dusty Miller
Chrysanthemum ptarmiciflorum

Dusty miller is grown for its beautiful and long-lasting foliage, silvery white and velvety to the touch. Plant in full sun and rich soil. Blooms in the summer; pinch flowers to keep the plant full and compact. Good in containers. Perennial in mild climates.

Four-O'Clock
Mirabilis jalapa

An old-time favorite, the trumpet-like flowers of the four o'clock open in the late afternoon, releasing their sweet scent. This 2–3 ft. plant comes in a variety of colors and bicolors. It is free-blooming, easy and undemanding in almost any soil in full sun or part shade.

Forget-Me-Not
Myosotis sylvatica

This lovely spring favorite is one of the truest blues in the garden. Low growing—to 12 in. tall—the forget-me-not is excellent for bedding or as a carpet under spring bulbs. Sow outdoors in early fall for blossoms next spring or start indoors. Performs best in moist soil and partial shade. Reseeds freely.

Gazania
Gazania rigens

Available in many colors and varieties that grow to 1–3 ft., gazania is perfect for edging, beds or containers. Considered a perennial in mild climates, it is often used as a groundcover. Plant in full sun, in light, sandy soil; it prefers hot, dry areas. Flowers close on cloudy days and at night.

ANNUAL PLANT GALLERY

Geranium
Pelargonium x hortorum

Great for containers, window boxes, beds and borders with abundant blooms in red, pink, salmon, violet, white or double varieties, and some with foliage of various colors. Plant in sun or light shade in rich, moist soil; grows to 18–24 in. tall. Fertilize regularly and cut off spent flowers. Perennials in frost-free areas. Hybrids are easily grown from seed for large display beds.

Gloriosa Daisy
Rudbeckia hirta

This striking daisy was developed from the wild black-eyed Susan. Stems up to 3 ft. tall bear profuse blossoms in rich yellows and oranges during summer months. This annual is easy to grow, doing best in full sun. It will tolerate poor soils and is drought resistant. It is often grown as a short-lived perennial. Good cut flower.

Geranium, Trailing
Pelargonium peltatum

This longer, base-branching geranium is perfect for trailing over the edge of a window box, container or hanging basket. It is also available in a mix of red, pink, magenta, lavender and white flowers. Large flower heads bloom all summer. No need to pinch; care same as geranium.

Globe Amaranth
Gomphrena globosa

Keeping its color and form indefinitely, globe amaranth is one of the best dried flowers. Varieties range in size from 8 in. to 2 ft., and all have clover-like blooms. This is an easy, pest-free plant; it likes the sun and will tolerate drought, yet also does well in humid, windy and rainy conditions. It grows in almost any soil.

Gypsophila
Gypsophila elegans

Also known as baby's breath, gypsophila is usually seen in white but also comes in pink, lavender and red. The small, airy blooms rest on strong stems in summer and fall. Sow seeds directly into the garden. This plant prefers full sun and alkaline soil but will tolerate poor soils except for heavy clay. Excellent cut flower.

Godetia
Clarkia amoena

Godetia is known for its showy, cup-shaped flowers in white, salmon-pink, lilac-crimson and other bicolors. Sow directly into the garden, as this annual does not transplant well. Place in full sun and well-drained soil and keep moist. In hotter climates, godetia does best in light shade. Dwarf varieties are excellent for bedding.

Heliotrope
Heliotropium arborescens

Heliotrope is most prized for the delicious fragrance of its purple, lilac and white flowers. The plants grow to 18–24 in. high in full sun or light shade. Sow in fertile, moist soil with good drainage. This annual is particularly effective near windows, walks and patios where its perfume can be enjoyed. Good for containers and for cut flower bouquets.

Impatiens, New Guinea

Impatiens New Guinea Hybrids

Developed from species native to New Guinea, this plant offers attractive foliage often striped with cream, red or yellow. The large flowers come in lavender, red, orange, pink, rose and purple. Plants range from 8 in. to 2 ft. and can tolerate sun better than other impatiens. Provide them with plenty of water and fertilizer.

Impatiens

Impatiens wallerana

Because of its mounds of ever-blooming flowers, impatiens is the best annual for shaded areas. It grows 1–2 ft. tall, depending on the variety, and rewards gardeners with nonstop color on plants that require a minimum of attention. Impatiens performs best in cool, moist soil. Numerous seed strains are available in sizes ranging from dwarfs—under 8 in. tall—to tall forms that grow to 24 in.; most colors are available except blue and yellow, and many have striped petals.

Impatiens, double

Impatiens wallerana 'Rosette' hybrids

This stunning variety has double flowers that resemble tiny rosebuds and open into peach, purple, red, white and lavender flowers. Double impatiens don't produce as many flowers as singles, but work quite well in containers. Some varieties have variegated gray-green leaves edged in creamy white.

Johnny-Jump-Up
Viola tricolor

A delicate, multi-colored flower with a cheerful face describes this viola, which grows on small 6–12 in. tufted plants. Like miniature pansies, it comes in purple, yellow, blue, lavender, mauve and apricot. Sow these spring-blooming plants in a woodland garden or to fill a container. They self-sow in later seasons.

Lavatera
Lavatera trimestris

A bold, striking plant, similar to hibiscus, with 4 in. blooms in shades of rose and white. Plant directly into the garden, in full sun, and lavatera will bloom continuously until frost. For best results, remove spent blooms and keep well watered and fertilized.

Larkspur
Consolida ambigua

An elegant flower, larkspur has single or double blooms on tall tapering spikes 2–4 ft. high in white, pink, blue and purple. It performs best in cool weather, making it an excellent spring flower for warm regions. Plant in full sun, in moist, well-drained soil. Deadhead for extra blooms and stake if necessary. Good cut and dried flower.

Linum
Linum grandiflorum

Often called flowering flax, this dainty flower grows up to 15 in. high. It has 1 in. blooms during summer and fall that resemble buttercups lasting only one day but are replenished quickly. Flowers come in many colors but most renowned is the brilliant scarlet. Likes full sun and well-drained soil.

ANNUAL PLANT GALLERY

Marigold, African
Tagetes erecta

The African marigold is known for its very large chrysanthemum-like flowers—as much as 5 in. in diameter. This is a strong, bold plant which grows from 1 1/2–3 ft. high and never needs staking. It thrives in full sun. Fine cut flower.

Lobelia
Lobelia erinus

Lobelia is a low, compact or trailing plant whose flowers come in vivid purple and blue as well as reddish purple, pink and white. Blooms are dainty—only 1/2 in. across—but they cover the 4–8 in. plant all season long until frost. Some strains are upright and compact and good for edging; others are trailing and among the best for hanging baskets. Plant in sun or part shade and keep soil moist or mulch around plants. Rich, fertile soil will produce vigorous plants. If plants get leggy, cut back.

Marigold, French Double
Tagetes patula

The French marigold ranges from 6–12 in. high in radiant oranges, yellows, reds and bicolors. It is a showy little plant that is trouble-free and blooms profusely all season. Use it for mass plantings, edging plants, window boxes or containers. Heat tolerant and easy to grow.

Marigold, French Single
Tagetes patula

The single French marigold is a reliable garden performer offering many bright blossoms in yellow, orange, or mahogony; some varieties are bicolored. It is easy to start from seed and flowers over a long period. Keep faded blooms pinched off to extend blooming.

Nemophila
Nemophila menziesii

Known as baby blue eyes, this old-fashioned favorite produces an abundance of sky-blue shallow-cupped flowers 6–8 in. high. It flourishes where summers are cool. Plant in sun or part shade, in moist, well-drained soil. Grows in compact mounds and is good for edgings.

Nasturtium
Tropaeolum majus

Easy to grow, long-blooming and brilliantly colored, the nasturtium is a bushy, spreading, lightly scented annual that does well in virtually any soil. Sow directly where it is to grow, in sun or part shade. Blooms in summer and fall. Excellent for foregrounds in beds and borders.

Nicotiana
Nicotiana species

A traditional favorite, nicotiana has trumpet-shaped flowers. Hybrids are compact, growing 2–3 ft. high in a variety of colors. *N. sylvestris* and *N. alata* are old-fashioned, extremely fragrant species that grow 3–4 ft. tall with 3 in. blooms. Plant in sun or part shade near a window or porch to enjoy the fragrance. Pick off spent blossoms and keep moist.

Annual Plant Gallery

Nigella
Nigella damascena

This charming, old-fashioned annual is often called love-in-a-mist. The 2 ft. plant resembles bachelor's buttons, and is available in blue, pink and white flowers framed by airy, delicate foliage. Sow in sun directly where they are to grow and sow again 3–4 weeks later to extend bloom. Good dried flower.

Nierembergia
Nierembergia hippomanica violacea

Also known as the cup flower, this plant forms a pretty purple mound with deep green, finely divided foliage and grows 6–12 in. high in summer. The blue to violet flowers are bell-shaped, 1 in. across. With its spreading habit, it is useful as edging or border material. Give it full sun in cool regions, protection in hot and dry areas. Trim it back after flowering for a neater look.

Pansy
Viola wittroskiana

This sweet-faced favorite has something for everyone. Available in a multitude of colors and bicolors, it has delicate small flowers or large ones up to 4 in. across. It provides continuous spring color. New varieties tolerate heat, but most do best in part shade. Keep faded flowers picked and pinch back for bushier growth. The flowers and leaves are easy to press or dry for use in beautiful lasting arrangements.

Petunia, Hybrid Grandflora
Petunia x *hybrida*

The petunia comes in a rainbow of colors and bicolors. It grows up to 15 in. high and thrives in full sun or light shade with moist soil. Grandiflora varieties have the largest flowers, which reach 4 in. across. Cascading varieties are good for hanging baskets.

Petunia, Hybrid Double
Petunia x *hybrida*

With its many showy, ruffled petals, the double petunia looks like a large carnation. Its frilly flowers come in a wide range of colors including white, blue, purple, pink and bicolors. The double petunia is available as both the grandiflora and multiflora varieties.

Petunia, Hybrid Multiflora
Petunia x *hybrida*

This petunia has smaller flowers but produces them in great quantities. It is unexcelled in mass plantings and is slightly more vigorous than other petunias. Use it in beds, borders or containers. As with all petunias, pinch back spent flowers for more blooms. Cut back late in the season to remove leggy growth and encourage new growth. Multiflora varieties hold up well in rainy climates.

Phlox
Phlox drummondii

The multicolored flowers of phlox are delicate, yet plants are hardy, heat-resistant and easy to grow. Plant phlox in full sun; it will withstand long, hot summers. Dwarf varieties are 8 in. tall; others reach up to 15 in. in height. Fertilize regularly for best results. Fragrant at dusk. Excellent cut flower.

ANNUAL PLANT GALLERY

Poppy, Iceland
Papaver nudicaule

This poppy is elegant, graceful and easy to grow. Flowers are yellow, cream orange or pink, single or double. Plants will grow to 12–18 in. tall. Sow directly into the garden, in full sun. The Iceland poppy does best in cool conditions; in warm areas it will be a perennial. It is one the best choices for winter color in warm winter climates; set out in early fall. Excellent cut flower.

Poppy, Shirley
Papaver rhoeas

The red variety of the Shirley poppy is the poppy of Flander's field. Flowers also come in pink, orange and white, dazzling in the sunlight on 2–5 ft. tall stems. Sow directly into the garden every few weeks for successive bloom. This poppy performs well in sun and hot weather and prefers light, well-drained soil. Protect from wind.

Portulaca
Portulaca grandiflora

Portulaca is also called moss rose because its sweet flower looks much like a miniature rose in shades of pink, red, yellow and white. Nothing can beat this low-growing succulent in hot, dry areas. It forms a 5 in. dense carpet in full sun and light soil and needs very little maintenance. Blooms in summer and fall.

Salpiglossis
Salpiglossis sinuata

Salpiglossis is known for its unusual lily-like, trumpet-shaped blooms with dark contrasting veins that look like they are made of velvet. It flowers in summer and fall and will reach 3 ft. high in full sun and rich, moist soil. It flourishes where summers are cool. Does best with slow-release fertilizer. Good cut flower.

Salvia
Salvia farinacea

Salvia farinacea is known for its striking 1–3 ft. spires which are profusely covered with blue, purple or white flowers. This plant needs full sun and is especially tolerant of heat and humidity. Grow in masses for effective color during summer and fall.

Salvia
Salvia splendens

Bearing bold flower spikes, salvia splendens grows to 1–3 ft. with an abundance of blooms to frost. Flowers come in pink, red, white and purple. It makes an excellent bedding plant and works well in borders and containers. Plant in sun or light shade, preferably in rich soil. Keep well watered and fertilized. Red-flowered varieties attract hummingbirds.

Scabiosa
Scabiosa atropurpurpea

The showy flower of scabiosa has tiny, silver stamens that resemble pins stuck in a pincushion. Blossoms can be pink, blue, red, white or dark purple on 3 ft. stems. They attract bees and butterflies. Sow seeds directly in full sun and rich soil. Excellent cut or dried flower. Reseeds.

ANNUAL PLANT GALLERY

Statice
Limonium sinuatum

Statice is one of the best everlasting flowers. Full, graceful sprays of delicate, papery blossoms in blue, lavender, pink, yellow and white top stiff stems. Plants grow to 2 1/2 ft. in full sun during summer and fall. Water only as needed. Superb cut flower.

Stock
Matthiola incana

A wonderfully fragrant plant, stock has luxuriant blooms on tall spikes to 3 ft. high. Most are double blooms in pink, red, blue, purple and white. A cool-weather plant, it is best in spring and early summer. Plant in sun or light shade, in a cool location and rich soil. Dwarf stock blooms earlier and often performs better in warmer regions. Good cut flower.

Snapdragon
Antirrhinum majus

Snapdragon's spikes of vivid color provide abundant bloom from summer through frost. Tall and intermediate varieties, up to 3 ft. tall, provide an important vertical line in the border. Dwarf varieties only 6–10 in. tall work well as edging for the border. Plant in full sun or light shade, in loose rich soil. The snapdragon will often winter over in warmer climates. It is, however, susceptible to rust and mildew problems—avoid overhead watering and plant rust-resistant varieties. Excellent cut flower.

Strawflower

Helichrysum bracteatum

The most popular of the everlasting flowers, the strawflower has showy papery flowers in a wide range of brilliant colors. It grows to 3 ft. high in full sun and slightly sandy soil and is heat tolerant. Excellent dried flower; to dry, cut just before center petals open.

Swan River Daisy

Brachycome iberidifolia

A profuse bloomer that deserves to be grown more often, the Swan River daisy grows to 15 in. high and produces masses of fragrant daisy-like flowers in blue or pink. Sow in sun and rich moist soil. Plant successively every 3–4 weeks to prolong bloom. Excellent for edging or massing.

Sunflower

Helianthus species

The sunflower is known for its very large, bright yellow flowers with dark centers. Plants come in a range of sizes from 3 to 10 ft. tall and have single or double flowers. Plant in full sun; endures heat well. Tall varieties will need staking. Sunflowers are easy and fun for children to grow. Good cut flower.

Sweet Sultan

Centaurea moschata

The sweet-scented fluffy flowers of the sweet sultan resemble those of the thistle. They can be purple, pink, yellow or white on a plant which reaches 2 ft. in height. Sow directly where they are to grow, and plant successively every few weeks to prolong bloom. Grows in full sun. Excellent cut flower.

Annual Plant Gallery

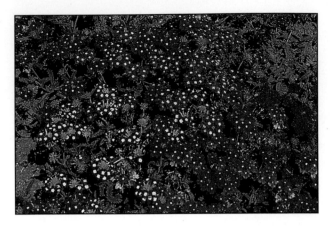

Verbena
Verbena x hybrida

Verbena comes in a rainbow of colors. Plants put on a stunning display of profuse blooms during summer months. Many flowers have an interesting white eye in the center. Upright and creeping varieties are available; most are 6–12 in. high. Plant in full sun in well-drained soil. Heat resistant.

Texas Bluebonnet
Lupinus texensis

Spikes of royal blue flowers tinged with white grace these 8–12 in. plants. Start seeds directly in garden in full sun and in soil with good drainage. This annual performs best in cool, humid weather; in hot areas, plant earlier and use as a spring flower. Great for naturalizing.

Vinca
Catharanthus roseus

Also known as the Madagascar periwinkle, this ever-blooming plant thrives in many conditions from sun to shade, heat or humidity. It grows to 15 in. with flowers in bright, colorful hues of white, pink, purple and bicolors. Locate in sun or part shade. Needs warm soil.

Wishbone Flower
Torenia fournieri

A splendid, colorful bloomer for the shade, the wishbone flower has trumpet-shaped pink, blue or purple blossoms with yellow throats on 1 ft. plants. It is rapid growing and disease resistant. Plant in partial shade in rich, moist soil. This annual prefers cool weather. Use for edging, in beds or pots. Pinch back for bushier plants.

Zinnia, Classic
Zinnia angustifolia 'Classic'

For a compact plant good in hanging baskets or borders, try the classic zinnia. Plants reach 8–12 in. tall and spread to 2 ft. The narrow leaves set off the many orange 1 in. flowers that continue to bloom late in the season. Blooms appear 6 weeks after seeds are sown.

Zinnia, Dahlia Flowered
Zinnia elegans

The zinnia is one of the most popular annuals because it is easy to grow and gives continuous bloom all season long. Flowers come in all colors except blue. Typically, this zinnia reaches 1 1/2 ft. and has 3 in. flowers. Taller varieties grow to 4 ft. and smaller kinds reach only 1 ft. Sow seeds directly in the garden. Excellent as a cut flower.

Zinnia, Cactus Flowered
Zinnia elegans

Unlike other zinnia flowers, the cactus and giant cactus zinnias have striking quilled petals on flowers reaching 7 in. The plants grow to 2 ft. and thrive in summer heat; water generously (at ground level) and fertilize.

ANNUAL VINES

Vines have a special place in the garden. They produce abundant flowers in a minimum of space and soften or even hide harsh objects. Grow them along fences or walls, on lampposts or railings. Plant vines six to eight inches away from their support. Dig a hole at least one foot wide and one feet deep and add plenty of organic matter.

Clockvine
Thunbergia gregorii

Clockvine is a vigorous plant that will grow quickly and easily in hanging baskets, on trellises or fences, or as a groundcover. Sow in sun or part shade. Bright orange flowers are produced nearly year-around in mild winter areas where it is a perennial. Roots survive brief freezes.

Climbing Nasturtium
Tropaeolum majus

The nasturtium is trailing or dwarf and compact. Look for a variety that is trailing, and you will have an excellent plant for trellises and fences. Flowers are fragrant, in bright yellows and oranges. Plant in sun or partial shade, directly where they are to grow. It will tolerate most any soil.

Hyacinth Bean
Dolichos lablab

The hyacinth bean is one of the fastest growing vines. It produces spikes of purple or white pea-like flowers which are followed by red beans. Sown directly in full sun and well-drained soil, it will grow to 10 ft. in height. It is perennial in warm climates.

Moonflower
Ipomoea alba

This spectacular vine has large white flowers up to 5–6 in. across that open at dusk and release a wonderful perfume. Plant in full sun. This is a vigorous climber but it will need support. To appreciate it fully, plant it near a porch, window or patio. Intermix with morning glories, and you will have blooms both day and night.

Scarlet Runner Bean
Phaseolus coccineus

This is a fast-growing vine, up to 15 ft. in height, with showy scarlet flowers followed by edible beans. Plant in full sun and provide plenty of water. It will need poles or other support in order to climb. Also available in white.

Morning Glory
Ipomea purpurea

Large trumpet-shaped flowers make the morning glory the most popular of vines. It can provide quick color on fences, porches or trellises. Flowers come in vivid blues and purples, but also scarlet and white. In full sun, this vine will reach 10 ft. tall. It is also available in dwarf varieties for bedding.

Sweet Pea
Lathyrus odoratus

One of the sweetest scented annuals, these colorful, climbing plants typically grow over fences and trellises. The sweet pea generally does best in cool areas, but look for heat-resistant varieties for warm zones. Sow directly in rich soil, full sun. Mulch and keep watered. Also available in knee-high or non-climbing varieties.

BIENNIALS

ANNUAL OR BIENNIAL

A biennial is a plant that completes its life cycle in two years. The first year it produces leaf growth. The second year, the plant blooms, produces seed and dies.

Some of our most treasured flowers are biennials, but many people don't want to wait for plants that take two years to bloom. Plants such as hollyhocks and foxgloves are most certainly worth the effort.

The traditional method of sowing biennials is to start them the year before blooms are desired. Sow seeds in mid summer in Zones 3–6, in early to mid fall in Zones 7–8, and in late fall or early winter in Zones 9–10. Start them in flats or sow directly into the garden. If you are starting them in late summer, give seedlings some shade until established, then move them to their sunny position. Where winters are cold, be sure and provide winter protection.

If started early, some biennials can actually flower the first year. Hollyhocks, for example, can be started indoors in February or early March, and they will bloom in mid to late summer until frost.

Once established, many biennials reseed themselves freely. To ensure blooms and the colors you prefer, however, it is best to plant new seeds each year.

Anchusa
Anchusa capensis

Tiny sky-blue flowers resembling forget-me-nots grow in abundant clusters on this biennial. Their color is one of the most vivid floral blues. Plant in full sun, preferably where evenings are cool. Provide soil with good drainage and keep plants moist. Cut back after bloom for continuous flowering.

Canterbury Bell
Campanula medium

These charming, bell-shaped flowers are an old-fashioned favorite. Easily grown from seed, most newer varieties will flower the first year if started indoors early. Flowers come in blue, purple, lavender and pink on plants that grow 1–3 ft. tall. Sow in sun or part shade, in rich soil. May need staking.

Foxglove
Digitalis purpurea

An elegant and stately plant, foxglove produces tall floral spires, reaching 4 ft. in height, in yellow, cream, pink and purple. It can flower the first year, 5 months after seeds are sown, so start in February for June blooms. It prefers part shade and rich, moist soil.

Sweet William
Dianthus barbatus

This bright, cheerful flower is indispensable in the garden for edging, bedding or in containers. Tight clusters of blooms look like miniature bouquets and come in numerous colors and bicolors. Many varieties bloom the first year. Provide sun and well-drained, rich soil.

Hollyhock
Alcea rosea

An excellent choice for the back of the border, the hollyhock has blooms on tall spires up to 8 ft. in height. Flowers come in single or double forms and in most colors except blue. If started early, it will bloom the first year. Plant in full sun and rich soil, and water and fertilize regularly.

Wallflower
Cheiranthus cheiri

This sweet-scented flower forms numerous clusters on 2 ft. stems. It comes in a wide variety of colors and is often seen in shades of yellow and orange. Plant in sun or part shade. Most varieties prefer cool weather, but *C. allionii* is heat tolerant. Sow early for flowers the first year.

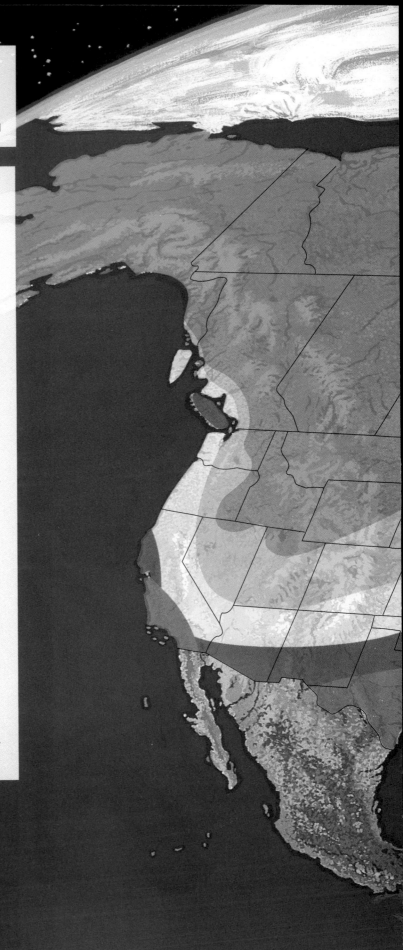

ANNUAL PLANTING ZONES

WHEN TO PLANT

Annuals are classified into three groups based on the conditions needed for growth: *hardy*, *half-hardy* and *tender*.

Hardy annuals can survive several mild frosts and their seeds can be planted in the early spring as soon as soil becomes workable. Some can be planted in the fall for winter or early spring flowering.

Half-hardy annuals can survive mild frosts but should be planted after danger of heavy frosts. Half-hardy annuals are often called cool-weather annuals because they can survive cool-weather and the soil temperature does not have to be high for germination.

Tender annuals should be planted in warm soil in early spring. These warm-weather annuals are very susceptible to frost. Both half-hardy annuals and tender annuals are often started indoors.

Find your location on the planting zone map shown here. Plant your annuals outdoors within the time period indicated on the key.

These are merely general guidelines. Each respective area of the country has many different factors that affect climates and all have *microclimates*, or pockets that are affected by wind, rain or other weather patterns that cannot be mapped. The best and most precise information will come from your state Agricultural Extension Service.

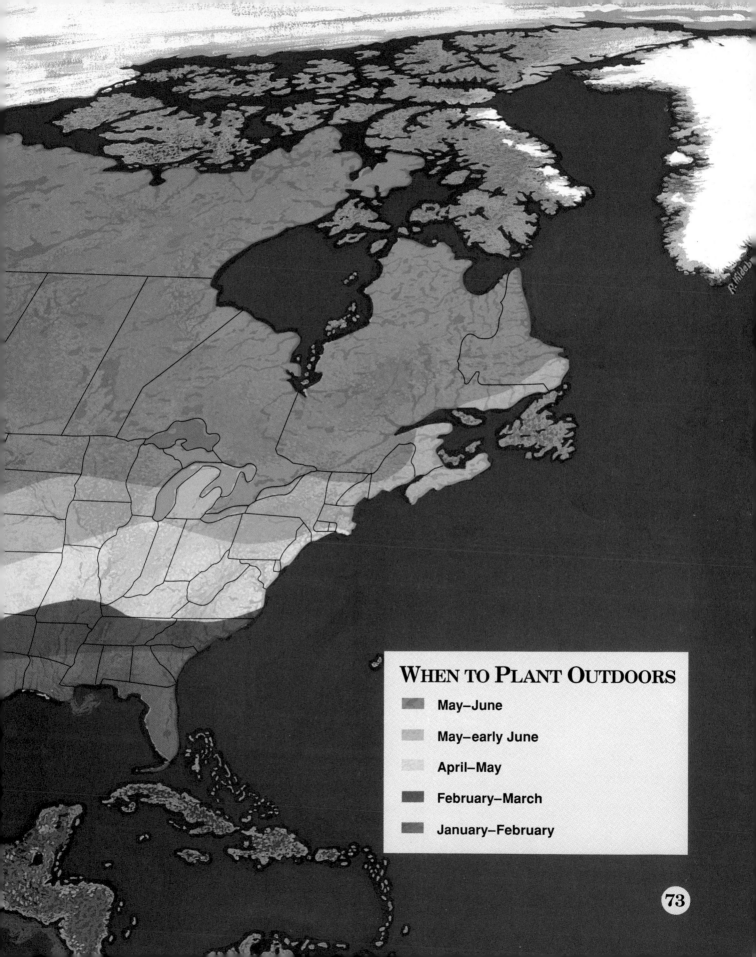

WHEN TO PLANT OUTDOORS

May–June

May–early June

April–May

February–March

January–February

PLANT DATA CHART

Everything needed to plant annuals is found here, from characteristics to light requirements. Use this table as a handy reference.

Common Name	Hardy	Light	Height	Spread	Days to Germinate	When to Sow	Bloom Season	Red	Pink	Orange	Yellow
African Daisy	T	S	4–12"	12"	10–14	A, C	Su–F		X	X	X
Ageratum	T	S, PS	6–12"	9–12"	7–10	A, C	Su–F		X		
Alyssum, Sweet	H	S, PS	4–6"	12"	8–15	A, B	Su–F		X		
Amaranthus	T	S	3–5'	2'	8–10	C	Su	X			X
Balsam	T	S, PS	1–3'	1–2'	8–14	A, C, D	Sp–F	X	X		X
Bachelor's Button	H	S	1–3'	1'	7–14	B	Su–F	X	X		X
Begonia, Wax	T	PS	6–12"	6–12"	14–20	A	Su–F	X	X		
Bells of Ireland	T	S, PS	2–3'	1'	25–35	A, C	Mid Su–F				
Browallia	T	S, PS	12–18"	8–10"	14–21	A	Su–F				
Butterfly Flower	HH	S, PS	12–14"	12"	20–30	A	Sp, Su	X	X		X
Calendula	H	S	1–2'	1–2'	10–14	B, D	Sp–F			X	X
California Poppy	H	S	1'	1'	10–12	B, D	Sp–Su	X	X	X	X
Candytuft	H	S	8–14"	1'	5–14	A, B, D	Sp–F	X	X		
Carnation	H	S	1–2'	3–6"	14–21	A, C, D	Su–F	X	X		X
Celosia, Crested	T	S	6"–2'	6–12"	8–14	C	Su–F	X	X	X	X
Celosia, Plumed	T	S	6"–2'	8–12"	8–14	C	Su–F	X	X	X	X
Chrysanthemum	H	S	8–10"	8–12"	10–15	A, B	Sp–Su				X
Cleome	HH	S, PS	3–6'	18–24"	5–14	A, C	Mid Su–F		X		
Coleus	T	S, PS	1'	2'	12	A, C	Sp–F				
Cosmos	HH	S	1–5'	1–3'	3–8	A, C	Su–F	X	X	X	X
Dahlberg Daisy	HH	S	4–6"	12"	10	A, C	Su				X
Dahlia	T	S	1–4'	1–3'	4–15	A, C	Su–F	X	X	X	X
Dianthus	HH	S	6–12"	6–12"	5–10	A, D	Su–F	X	X		
Dusty Miller	HH	S	6–24"	8–12"	7–21	A, C, D	Su				
Forget-Me-Not	H	S, PS	6–12"	12"	14–21	A, B, D	Sp				
Four-o'Clock	HH	S, PS	2–3'	2'	7–10	A, C	Su	X	X		X
Gazania	HH	S	1–3'	12"	4–12	A, C	Su	X	X	X	X
Geranium	T	S	10–24"	12–24"	7–15	A	Su–F	X	X	X	
Geranium, Trailing	T	S	2–6'	Up to 36"	7–15	A	Su–F	X	X	X	
Globe Amaranth	T	S	6–30"	18–24"	14	A, C	Su–F	X	X	X	X
Gloriosa Daisy	H	S	2–3'	2'	5–10	A, B	Su			X	X
Godetia	H	S, PS	1–2'	1'	10–15	B, D	Su–F	X	X		
Gypsophila	H	S	1–2'	2'	10	A, C	Su–F	X	X		
Heliotrope	T	S, PS	1–2'	12–15"	7–21	A	Su–F				
Impatiens	T	PS	1–3'	Up to 3'	15–20	A, C	Su–F	X	X	X	
Johnny–Jump–Up	H	S, PS	4–12"	4–12"	10–20	A, B, D	Sp–Su				X
Larkspur	H	S	2–4'	2'	10–20	A, D	Su		X		X
Lavatera	H	S	3–4'	2'	7–21	C	Mid Su–F		X		
Linum	HH	S	12–15"	12"	12–15	B, D	Su–F	X	X		
Lobelia	HH	S, PS	4–8"	6"	15–20	A	Su–F	X	X		
Marigold	T	S	6"–3'	Up to 2'	7	A, C	Su–F	X		X	X
Nasturtium	HH	S, PS	1'	2'	10–14	A, C	Su–F	X	X	X	X

Blue	Purple	White	Multi-color	Frag-rance	Cut-flower	Ever-lasting	Con-tainer	Hanging Basket	Poor Soil	Comments
		X			X		X			Endures heat and drought
X		X					X	X	X	Good for edging; pinch back; self sows
	X	X		X			X	X	X	Good for edging; self-sows
			X						X	Sow directly; colorful foliage
	X	X					X			Good for part shade
X	X	X			X					Sow successively; endures heat
		X	X				X	X		Difficult to start from seed
					X					Tall green spires; soak seeds
X	X	X					X	X		Easy; prefers part shade
	X	X	X		X		X			Needs cool summers
					X		X			Easy; sow second planting for fall flowers
		X							X	Sow directly; endures drought
	X	X	X				X			Compact and low growing; endures heat
	X	X	X	X	X		X			Pinch back for bushier growth
	X				X	X	X			Good for late summer and fall
	X				X	X	X			Keep deadheaded
		X					X	X		Does best in cool conditions
	X	X			X				X	Tall, excellent for border; endures heat
			X				X	X		Excellent foliage plant; prefers cool shade
	X	X			X				X	Open, sprawling plant
					X		X	X	X	Easy; long bloomer; low growing
	X	X	X		X		X			Excellent bedding plant; keep mulched
	X	X	X	X		X	X		X	Good for edging; new cultivars heat resistant
							X			Foliage plant; pinch back for bushier growth
X							X	X		Prefers cool, moist soil, part shade
		X	X	X					X	Easy; very fragrant; self sows
		X	X				X			Endures heat, drought and wind
		X	X				X	X		Easy; water regularly; good for containers
		X	X				X	X		Try in a window box
	X	X			X	X	X		X	Endures heat, humidity and wind
					X				X	Likes hot summers
	X	X	X						X	Sow directly; likes cool, dry climate
	X	X			X	X			X	Plant successively for extra blooms
	X	X		X	X		X			Fragrant; bushy and compact
	X	X					X	X		Shade lover; water well
X	X						X	X		Best in cool summer regions
X	X	X			X	X				Deadhead; water well
		X			X					Sow directly; self-sows
X	X								X	Likes cool climates
X	X	X					X	X		Good for edging; doesn't tolerate heat well
		X	X		X		X		X	Easy to grow
		X		X			X	X	X	Easy; water well; do not fertilize

Common Name	Hardy	Light	Height	Spread	Days to Germinate	When to Sow	Bloom Season	Red	Pink	Orange	Yellow
Nemophila	HH	S, PS	6–8"	7–9"	5–10	A, B	Su–F				
Nicotiana	T	S, PS	10"–4'	6"–2'	10–20	A, C	Sp–Su	X	X		
Nierembergia	T	S, PS	6–12"	6–12"	14–21	A	Su–F				
Nigella	H	S	12–24"	8–12"	8–16	B, D	Su–F		X		
Pansy	H	S, PS	6–8"	6"	10–20	A, B, D	Sp–Su	X	X	X	X
Petunia	T	S	12–15"	12–24"	7–10	A	Su–F	X	X		X
Phlox	T	S	8–15"	8"	6–15	A, B, D	Su–F	X	X		
Poppy, Iceland	H	S	12–18"	12"	6–14	B, D	Su	X	X	X	X
Poppy, Shirley	H	S	2–3'	1'	10–15	B, D	Su	X	X	X	
Portulaca	T	S	6"	12"	10–15	A, C	Su–F	X	X	X	X
Salpiglossis	T	S	2–3'	1'	4–12	A, C	Su–F	X	X	X	X
Salvia splendens	T	S	10–36"	10–24"	12–15	A, C	Su–F	X	X		
Salvia farinacea	T	S	24–36"	2'	12–15	A, C	Su–F				
Scabiosa	HH	S	2–3'	2'	15–20	A, C	Su–F	X	X		
Snapdragon	HH	S, PS	6–36"	8–12"	5–12	A, B	Su–F	X	X	X	X
Statice	HH	S	2'	2'	6–18	A, C	Su–F		X		X
Stock	H	S, PS	12–36"	12"	8	A, C, D	Su–F	X	X		
Strawflower	HH	S	12–36"	12–15"	7–10	A, C	Su–F	X	X	X	X
Sunflower	HH	S	3–10'	8–12"	3–7	C	Su–F			X	X
Swan River Daisy	HH	S	10–15"	6–12"	15–20	A, C	Su		X		
Sweet Sultan	H	S	2'	1'	7–10	C, D	Su		X		X
Texas Bluebonnet	HH	S	8–12"	10–12"	10–15	B, C, D	Sp				
Verbena	HH	S	6–12"	2'	20–25	A	Su	X	X		
Vinca	T	S, PS	8–15"	10–12"	15–20	A	Su–F		X		
Wishbone Flower	T	PS	8–12"	8"	15–20	A, C	Su–F		X		
Zinnia	T	S	6"–4'	6–12"	3–7	A, C	Su–F	X	X	X	X
Vines											
Climbing Nasturtium	HH	S, PS	6–10'	6'	10–14	A, C	Su–F	X	X	X	X
Clockvine	HH	S, PS	Up to 6'	6'	5–12	A, C	Late Su–F			X	X
Hyacinth Bean	H	S	10'	12"	14	A, C	Su–F				
Moonflower	T	S	15'	6"	10	A, C	Su				
Morning Glory	HH	S	Up to 10'	6"	8–10	A, C	Su	X	X		
Scarlet Runner Bean	T	S	8–15'	3–6"	8–12	C	Su	X			
Sweet Pea	H	S	Up to 5'	1'	10–14	A, B, D	Sp–Su	X	X		
Biennials											
Anchusa	HH	S	10–18"	10"	6–16	A, B, D	Su–F				
Canterbury Bell	H	S, PS	1–3'	1–1 1/2'	15–20	A	Su		X		
Foxglove	H	PS	3–4'	1'	7–14	A, B	Su	X	X		X
Hollyhock	HH	S	Up to 10'	2–3'	5–18	A	Su	X	X	X	X
Sweet William	HH	S	4–24"	12–18"	8	A, B, D	Su–F	X	X		
Wallflower	H	S, PS	2'	1'	5–7	A, B, D	Sp–Su	X		X	X

Blue	Purple	White	Multi-color	Frag-rance	Cut-flower	Ever-lasting	Con-tainer	Hanging Basket	Poor Soil	Comments
X							X			Compact mounds; good for edging
		X		X	X		X			Endures humidity
	X						X			Trim after bloom for neater look
X		X			X					Plant successively for additional blooms
X	X	X	X		X		X	X		Chill seeds; good for mass plantings
X	X	X	X				X	X	X	Pinch back for bushier growth
	X	X		X	X		X			Easy; plant successively; endures heat
		X			X					Likes cool, sunny conditions
	X	X			X				X	Hairy stems and buds; great red
	X	X					X		X	Excellent for hot, dry locations
X	X				X					Sensitive to fertilizer; use slow release
	X	X			X		X			Tolerates part shade
X	X	X								Endures heat and humidity
X	X	X		X	X					Attracts hummingbirds
		X	X		X					Pinch back for bushier plants
X	X	X			X	X				Excellent dried flower
X	X	X		X	X					Fragrant
	X	X			X	X				Open, loose form; excellent dried flower
					X					Endures heat and drought; attracts birds
X		X		X	X		X			Open, loose form; sow successively
	X	X		X	X					Deadhead
X										Naturalizes in milder climates
X	X	X		X	X		X	X		Endures heat; prone to mildew
	X	X	X				X	X		Endures heat; excellent for desert areas
X	X	X	X				X	X		Good for shade; endures heat
	X	X	X		X		X			Sow directly; tolerates heat
		X	X				X	X	X	Do not fertilize
	X						X	X		Endures part shade
	X	X								Vigorous
		X		X						Excellent at dusk; soak seeds 24 hours
X	X	X								Endures heat; soak seeds 24 hours
		X								Rapid growing; good screen
X	X	X	X	X	X		X			Climber; keep roots mulched and cool
X										Keep moist; shear back for second bloom
X	X	X								Very showy; easy to transplant
	X	X		X						Elegant spires; do not mulch close to plant
	X	X								Tall; soak seeds; susceptible to rust
	X	X								Keep soil moist
	X			X	X				X	Prefers cool conditions

INDEX

A Note From NK Lawn and Garden Co.

For more than 100 years, since its founding in Minneapolis, Minnesota, NK Lawn and Garden has provided gardeners with the finest quality seed and other garden products.

We doubt that our leaders, Jesse E. Northrup and Preston King, would recognize their seed company today, but gardeners everywhere in the U.S. still rely on NK Lawn and Garden's knowledge and experience at planting time.

We are pleased to be able to share this practical experience with you through this ongoing series of easy-to-use gardening books.

Here you'll find hundreds of years of gardening experience distilled into easy-to-understand text and step-by-step pictures. Every popular gardening subject is included.

As you use the information in these books, we hope you'll also try our lawn and garden products. They're available at your local garden retailer.

There's nothing more satisfying than a successful, beautiful garden. There's something special about the color of blooming flowers and the flavor of home-grown garden vegetables.

We understand how special you feel about growing things—and NK Lawn and Garden feels the same way, too. After all, we've been a friend to gardeners everywhere since 1884.